Silk:

Meditations on T'ai-Chi Ch'uan
& Other Poems

Silk:

Meditations on T'ai-Chi Ch'uan

& Other Poems

by

Morgan Grayce Willow

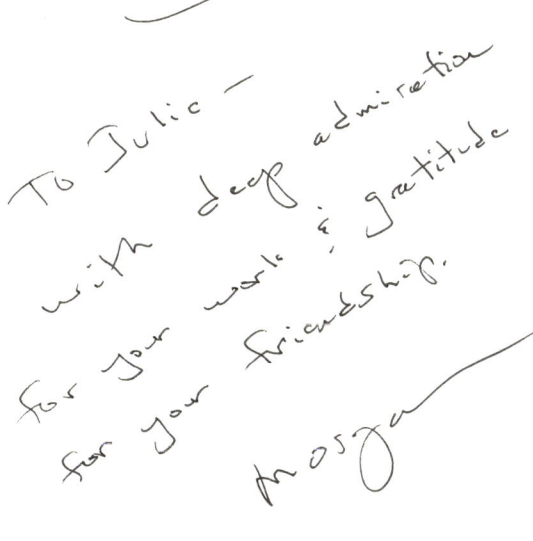

Shu-Kuang Press

Silk:
Meditations on T'ai-Chi Ch'uan & Other Poems

Copyright © 2009 Morgan Grayce Willow

ISBN 978-1-4276-4121-2
Published by Shu-Kuang Press
  PO 7876
  St. Paul, Minnesota 55107
  United States of America
  shukuangpress.com

Cover Calligraphy & Design by Todd Nesser

Author Photo: Rebecca Pavlenko

The author gratefully acknowledges the following publications in which some of these poems first appeared, in some cases in somewhat different versions: *Hurricane Alice, Wu Dang, Wee Wu Dang,* and *Arpeggio of Appetite* (Finishing Line Press, 2005).

Foreword

For more than twenty-five years, I learned the art of T'ai-Chi Ch'uan from Master T.T. Liang. Master Liang was the disciple of Professor Cheng Man-Ch'ing who was known as the "Master of Five Excellences," namely painting, poetry, calligraphy, medicine, and T'ai-Chi. Professor Cheng was also a master flower-arranger, musician, and chess player, going undefeated in Taiwan. My teacher many times praised Professor Cheng for his achievements in so many disciplines. Master Liang, himself, was a master of two: T'ai-Chi and calligraphy. While I mainly learned T'ai-Chi from him, he also taught me a lot about Chinese art and of the excellences.

I was surprised and overjoyed when the poet Morgan Grayce Willow came to my Studio to study T'ai-Chi. She came not only with a background in T'ai-Chi but also as a published and accomplished poet and teacher. She has generously shared her art with me and has written many poems, both inspired and requested, about Tai-Chi. She has led poetry workshops at our Twin Cities T'ai-Chi Ch'uan Studio annual retreats and has given seminars at our Studio, as well. It was at a retreat that Morgan began to write poems on her meditations concerning the poetic names of the T'ai-Chi postures.

The names of the movements in T'ai-Chi Ch'uan serve many purposes. They allude to the martial-art applications, point to outer or inner expressions of energy, describe the physical actions, and catalogue some of China's extensive history. Many of the names come from Taoism, Buddhism, and Chinese mythology sources.

By harmonizing these two excellences in her book *Silk*, Morgan shares her unique insights as poet and T'ai-Chi practitioner. Let these moving words influence your moving art.

Sifu Ray Hayward
Year of the Ox
2009

Preface

Silk: Meditations on T'ai-Chi Ch'uan is a collection of poetic meditations on the names of the postures in the Yang-style T'ai-Chi Ch'uan solo form and the Chinese characters from which those names are derived. My first inspiration is my practice of T'ai-Chi at Twin Cities T'ai-Ch'uan Studio under the direction of Sifu Ray Hayward and Sifu Paul Abdella. My second inspiration, and the source of my study of the characters, is *How to Grasp the Bird's Tail if You Don't Speak Chinese* by Jane Schorre, with calligraphy by Margaret Chang. In this book, Margaret Chang's beautiful characters are accompanied by Jane Schorre's translation, commentary, and etymological discussion. Shorre also relates fables and legends from Chinese mythology and folk lore that may have a bearing on the evolution of the characters.

My goal has been to capture an essence of each of the postures in poetic form. The poems are not meant to merely describe the postures or to instruct a reader in how to perform them; rather, they are meant to express one vision of an internal nature of each posture based on images inherent in the Chinese character. As with any language, Chinese characters have evolved over time, so sometimes I draw an image for a poem from an ancient form of the character. Since Chinese characters are ideographic by nature, these images resonate with the posture names even in translation, though most often not in a direct or literal way. Also, each poem is embedded in my experience of T'ai-Chi Ch'uan as an overarching metaphor for life. Like Lao Tzu's poems in *Tao Te Ching*, or *The Way of Life*, performing the solo form and studying the posture names has offered me guidance in how to live. In other words, T'ai-Chi Ch'uan is for me a spiritual practice. Poetry, also, is a spiritual practice. In *Silk*, these two practices converge.

This cycle of poems does, in fact, also draw some inspiration from Lao Tzu's *Tao Te Ching*. The specific translation that most moves me was done by the early Twentieth-Century American poet Witter Bynner, working in collaboration with Kiang Kang-hu. Though a somewhat less literal translation of the Tao than many, in Witter Bynner's version, each number in the sequence becomes an English poem in its own right. It's almost as though his true collaborator was the master himself. I imagine readers and listeners in Lao Tzu's time experiencing a resonance and simplicity of language in the original Chinese like that we experience from Witter Bynner's English.

The poetic form I chose for this series is the tanka, a 31-syllable, unrhymed Japanese form. The syllable count matches the following pattern:

> 1st line – 5 syllables,
> 2nd line – 7 syllables,
> 3rd line – 5 syllables,
> 4th line – 7 syllables,
> 5th line – 7 syllables.

Often, there is a turn or shift in imagery or intention between lines 3 and 4, though this is not a rigid requirement of the form. I chose this because, as with T'ai-Chi Ch'uan, I have learned that repeated practice of a specific form – along with the variation that each new day, new breath, or new intention brings – is illuminating. In other words, the form teaches me.

The Yang-style solo form as we practice it at Twin Cities T'ai-Chi Ch'uan Studio includes 150 postures. Many of these are repetitions. The poem cycle contains only one poem for each posture, regardless of how many times it is repeated in the form. Also, I have followed the order of the postures as laid out in the book by Jane Schorre and Margaret Chang. There are occasional variations in the English translation of posture names. I have tended to follow the name tradition that we use at the Studio; exceptions, however, occur when I found myself captivated by an image from an alternative translation. In this, I have followed a poet's, rather than a scholar's, sensibility. When an alternative translation has been particularly interesting, I have listed it in parentheses. Finally, I consulted a number of other texts while working on this series, and though it is unusual to include a bibliography in a collection of poems, I have done so. This is to acknowledge, at least in part, the debt I owe to many who came before me and to suggest possibilities for interested readers.

This project began for me as a practice, a way to study the art of poetry and the art of T'ai-Chi at the same time. The vision of it as a book came from Sifu Ray Hayward, and for this I am deeply grateful. In addition to the tanka series, Sifu reminded me of T'ai-Chi related poems I'd written over the years, some for special occasions within our practice community, others during our annual summer retreat. These are included in the second section of the collection. Many of these have appeared in our studio newsletter *Wu Dang*, and more recently, the online version, *Wee Wu Dang*. One of these poems, a tribute to Master T.T. Liang, hangs in our studio as a large banner. It's entirely due to Sifu's vision and enormous generosity of spirit that this book is coming into the world. For this reason — and for all the years of superlative teaching and unflagging enthusiasm — I dedicate this book to Sifu Ray Hayward.

Many people have contributed to the transformation of these poems from vision into book. I thank Todd Nesser for his lovely grass-style calligraphy of "silk" and for his stunning cover design. I also thank Todd for applying his impeccable standards to the design of the book as a whole. I thank Rondi Atkin who honored me by being first reader, editor, and meticulous proofreader for *Silk*; the text is better for it, though any errors are mine. My thanks to Mary Logue and Barbara Davis for reading the collection in manuscript and lending their remarks for the back cover. I thank Kim Hayward for marshaling the project from the first meeting agenda, through production, and out onto the website and into the world. In addition, I want to thank all the members of the Studio who have participated in my T'ai-Chi poetry workshops at the studio or during retreats, as well as those who have appreciated the poems in *Wu Dang* and *Wee Wu Dang*. Finally, my deepest gratitude to Blake Lynden for believing in me, as both poet and T'ai-Chi practitioner, all along.

Morgan Grayce Willow
April 2009

Contents

I

Prologue: Metamorphosis	2
Beginning Posture	3
Grasp Sparrow's Tail	4
Ward Off	5
Roll Back	6
Press	7
Push	8
Single Whip	9
Lift Hands	10
White Crane Spreads Its Wings	11
Brush Knee Twist Step	12
Play Guitar	13
Deflect Downward, Parry & Punch	14
Withdraw & Push (Apparent Close)	15
Cross Hands	16
Embrace Tiger, Return to Mountain	17
Fist Under Elbow	18
Repulse Monkey	19
Diagonal Flying	20
Needle at Sea Bottom	21
Fan through Back	22
Turn & Chop with Fist	23
Cloud Hands	24
High Pat on Horse	25
Separate Foot	26
Kick with Sole	27
Punch Downward	28
Kick Upward	29
Strike Tiger	30
Wind Pierces Ears	31
Parting Wild Horse's Mane	32
Fair Lady Weaving at the Shuttle	33
Snake Creeps Down	34
Golden Pheasant Stands on One Leg	35
White Snake Spits out Tongue	36

Thrusting Hand	37
Cross Kick	38
Punch to Groin	39
Step Forward to the Seven Stars	40
Step Back to Ride Tiger	41
Lotus Kick	42
Bend Bow, Shoot Tiger	43
Epilogue: The Tiger Way	44

II

The Value of Symmetry	47
Night of the Demons	48
Field of Cinnabar	52
Liang Meets Ana in the Afterlife	53
Sword Form	55
Morning T'ai-Chi	56
Bat	57
Oceans to Arches	58
Dicotyledon	59
Empty Stepping	60
Bibliography	62

I

Prologue: Metamorphosis

I become silkworm,
spiraling a single thread
around myself. *Chi.*
Cocoon. Protection. Ward off.
Evenly unwind: Issue.

Beginning Posture

To begin, I first
do nothing. Then like a tree,
I wait while Above
and Below both reach through me.
I become Mover and Moved.

Grasp Sparrow's Tail

Ordinary bird.
Dun-colored tail. Hold gently.
Observe. Each detail
contains *yin* and *yang*.
We play: whole body, whole mind.

Ward Off

One moon reflecting
on the surface of a lake:
two moons. When these friends
fly from each other, eddies
hold them, like arrow and bow.

Roll Back

Though waves rock a boat
back, passengers move forward.
Though oarsmen face past,
boat moves through time. Secrets of
the hand balance *yang* with *yin*.

Press

Slender, the stalk stands.
In cornfield, it is many
and yet always one.
Each stalk grows effortlessly,
drawing strength from root to tip.

Push

Flowers arranged for
an altar use space, color
shape. To issue *chi*,
first listen. Chrysanthemums
know how much color they need.

Single Whip

In flight, a bird's wings
and sinuous leather are
the same. Both transform
wind but are themselves unchanged.
One makes motion. One makes sound.

Lift Hands

Expand and open.
To stir up what is above,
we are given hands.
Practice, constant as sunrise,
strengthens sinew, stirs up skill.

White Crane Spreads Its Wings

White crane is dancing.
Each step among reeds empties.
From the muddy shore
to clouds, crane's luminous wings
deny gravity its reign.

Brush Knee Twist Step

To spin its cocoon,
a silkworm coils inside one
continuous thread.
To unspool the energy,
dance in smooth, steady spirals.

Play Guitar

I become pipa,
shape a hollow where music
comes from emptiness.
Commander and chariots
unite to become power.

Deflect Downward, Parry & Punch

What carries like a boat,
closes like a screen door slam,
thumps like a tree branch?
The hand. Accept what's given
to choose the circle's motion.

Withdraw & Push (Apparent Close)

A cunning person
seems to comply with great force
yet, like a willow
in fierce wind, turns the bluster
aside to bar its entrance.

Cross Hands

Again and again,
we move in four directions,
return to center.
As children, we learned to walk
always stopping and starting.

Embrace Tiger, Return to Mountain

Like a tiger cub,
I begin my journey with
wild energy. Held
close, but loosely, it carries
me up the mountain, and down.

Fist Under Elbow

A powerful wind
meets deeply rooted willow.
Tree trunk barely moves.
Branch nearest trunk moves little.
Yet farthest narrow tip snaps.

Repulse Monkey

Mirthful distracter,
monkey taunts my clever mind.
I reverse myself
to unwind accomplishments.
Unseen, I achieve my goal.

Diagonal Flying

White crane hatchling steps
in its mother's tracks, tests wings
again and again
before taking flight, repeats
her form before it can soar.

Needle at Sea Bottom

The strongest weapon
is small as monkey's needle
tucked behind his ear.
Mind intent, like his magic,
probes to the bottom of things.

Fan through Back

The doors of my spine
open. Light as feather, *chi*
rises. The blossom
of practice defeats all my
foes. Those within. Those without.

Turn & Chop with Fist

Turning the fabric
of life, we rip tattered cloth,
abandon what's done.
Shifting stance, hand like tree branch
drops through its portion of wheel.

Cloud Hands

Like the voice of earth,
vapor, raised by the sun's heat,
cools, scattering rain,
words from the clouds. Falling, they
alight, soft, yet strong as poems.

High Pat on Horse

When a child, I moved
easily as a young colt,
but now, I must strive
backward, untrain the circus
horse, let gravity teach me.

Separate Foot

Mind sharpened like knife
separates clear from unclear,
topples the weak thought.
Balance the far with the near
by thinking of the center.

Kick with Sole

If one rooted foot
obeys gravity, one foot
can climb a mountain.
Together, they separate.
The opponent cannot stand.

Punch Downward

The farmer who plants
seeds, first cuts a hole in earth.
From this wound, fruit grows.
Become skilled by losing first.
Many losses, many gains.

Kick Upward

An alert athlete
waits, patient as a lizard,
for his chance to move.
The swiftness of his motion
transforms the game's direction.

Strike Tiger

A hunter studies
the prowling tiger, listens
to the creature's heart.
In this way, she learns when to
step aside from tiger's path.

Wind Pierces Ears

On soft breezes, seeds
drift, populate plains with grass.
Every crevice filled.
In an instant, shifting winds
uproot ancient stands of trees.

Parting Wild Horse's Mane

Dust clouds deceive me.
Yet, slowly at first, practice
cuts through the tangles
to reveal strength in simple
movement, my heart's horse nature.

Fair Lady Weaving at the Shuttle

Delicate as lace,
a spider web connects four
directions. Its strength
is space. The fierce wasp is caught
when net suddenly appears.

Snake Creeps Down

Whip snaps. Snake strikes. Both
immediately recoil.
Flexibility
is strong as cutting edge of
plow stirring up what's below.

Golden Pheasant Stands on One Leg

In the golden dawn,
pheasant flies up from his nest,
one pure line of flight.
Solo bird and gravity
harmonize without effort.

White Snake Spits out Tongue

Relax like the snake
on sun-warmed boulder. Listen.
Vibrations will move
messages up from earth's core.
Shape them in words and body.

Thrusting Hand

I am the crossroad
between above and below,
the sum at center.
Four opposites converge here.
Yang always responds to *yin*.

Cross Kick

Meet the opponent
in the opponent's own house.
You walk together
under the same roof of sky.
Yin always responds to *yang*.

Punch to Groin

When hand points the way,
it is guided by the mind.
When mind leads the way,
train it to follow *tan t'ien*.
Then the target can be won.

Step Forward to the Seven Stars

Each star, like our sun,
gives birth to light. The seven
who make our Dipper
pin us to celestial realms.
Embrace those Heavenly Gates.

Step Back to Ride Tiger

Now the tiger cub
is all grown up; his antics
become sleek power.
With relaxed mind, we can ride
on his muscular shoulders.

Lotus Kick

Deep beneath lotus,
root at the bottom of pond,
unseen. When petals
unfold, one by one in turn,
the center moves not at all.

Bend Bow, Shoot Tiger

In the archer's hands:
bow, arrow, sinew, and space.
In the archer's mind,
nothing: neither target nor
intention. Just letting go.

Epilogue: The Tiger Way

To capture Tiger,
I step in each track again
and again, until
I've forgotten if Tiger
is before me or behind.

II

The Value of Symmetry

~ for Blake & T'ai-Chi Master, Cheng Man-Ch'ing

> what shoulder, & what art,
> Could twist the sinews of thy heart?
> *~ William Blake*

To stand in balance where two become three
I practice an art of timing: how release, when press.
The form itself teaches me.

If I become triangle, the bend of my knee
determines the angle my heart likes best
to stand in balance where two become three.

If I become sound, the poem decrees
which foot to tap, which vowel to stress.
The form itself teaches me.

When I am spine, my root energy
climbs the ladder, gives each rib a caress,
then arrives at balance where two become three.

If I become light, like a prism, I see
which colors to bend to weave the sun's dress.
The form itself teaches me.

If you were my lover, as I want you to be,
the dance we make as we step into guess
creates that balance where we two make three.
The form itself teaches me.

Night of the Demons

*A... life is limited whereas the calls
made upon it are not.*
   ~ Cheng Man-Ch'ing

All night they
came, out of the closets
of dark, marching
across the tundra
of my third eye. Their
large bodies, swayed, hairy
as mammoths, yet with
faces like those on stone
pillars, grimacing, bearing
teeth and tusks.
            I rose

and fell to the
thrumming of their
hooves, the whispers
of their strange
wings. Tumbled,
jarred I was no
rock to smooth
in their lapidary, no
clay to be fired
in their kiln. Yet
I rode the night
like a prince sitting
atop a rogue
elephant's head.

   They never graced
me with definite
forms. Nor
with names. Were there
seven? One
to do battle at each
chakra, one to prick
and pry at each stage
through my flesh, to reach
all the way back
to the snake coiled
along my spine. Fire

tortures for the
first three, water
tortures for the next
three, mounds and
mounds of earth
for the last, the
crown buried in tons
of murky soil. All

night I tossed.
The cats, the
thunderstorm, even
you a part
of the battle but not
clearly on
my side. Your
churnings through the smoky
air less to defend
me — or even
yourself — than simply
to pass through
this strange field, dark
as an orchard dotted
by burning smudge
pots on a night
of low clouds and no
wind. You passed
along one row. Beyond
reach.
    I saw
you. Held out
my hand. Even spoke.
But the demons grabbed
the words from
my tongue, forced
all air down
my throat till bitter
language slapped me
like low broken
branches.
       Morning,
though the sun

rose as if
there were nothing in
the air, though dew
formed on flowers, and
birds dared to speak
up, the demons
did not depart. They
wound themselves around
the light, wrapped
it up like skeins, doled
some out
      to me.

I walked gingerly,
knees bent, all
day. When the second
night fell, they
unwound from the
skein of day, laughing,
glad to be back, slapping
each other's broad
backs, taking my hair
into their hands, sliding
the strands along their
leathery palms, reading out
my secrets.
      Finally
I simply
refused to hear
them any
more. I gathered my knees,
my spine into the *tan t'ien*,
the sole place they had
not touched, and dropped
toward the center of the earth.
As I sank, my arms made wide
arcs to the right, to
the left. My
knees rose. Sparks leapt
from the soles of my feet
into their eyes. I grew

wings that spread
wide as an ocean, that
shed the demons' taunts
the way boulders shed
white waters. My round
embrace drew them
into me, then released
them like pebbles strewn
down a mountain side.
                      By dawn

of the third day
we were all
at rest. I sat
on my heels, round
as a clay bowl. My demons
scurried, small and busy
as ants, into a hole
in the middle
of the air.

Field of Cinnabar

~ *In memory of Master T. T. Liang*

His goal was to strengthen himself without interruption,
from desire, to intention, to first step — enticed
by the stream of a long river which rolls on.

Sick, reluctant to leave home, his birth nation,
Liang heeded a fortune teller's advice:
Seek to strengthen yourself without interruption.

His liver poisoned by a life of dissipation,
he sought T'ai-Chi Ch'uan, through practice
stepped into the stream, the long river which rolls on.

He learned to gather *ch'i*, to nurture its translation
through spine, to all movements — no deficiency, no excess.
In this way, he strengthened himself without interruption.

The teacher made ready; students asked for instruction.
Retired, yet not relieved from his calling, Liang passed
along his stream of that long river which rolls on.

Our practice honors his lifelong celebration.
His goal is ours: string pearls — no severance, no splice.
Having strengthened himself without interruption,
he continues. The stream, the long river rolls on.

Liang Meets Ana in the Afterlife
~ In memory of Ana Ortiz de Montellano

She is performing double knife
when he ambles over the hill.
She does not see him.
Her fury flashes off the blades.
Her face is set in concentration.
Her eyes are deep
and so full of rage
that no light can pass them now.

Master Liang pauses.
He does not advance.
His eyes gleam.
They carry more than enough light
for both of them.
The corners of his mouth are turned up slightly,
but his smile does not come from his mouth.
It comes from deep behind his face.

Ana, unaware of his presence,
steps through the formation.
She executes each posture precisely.
Only Master Liang sees the little frown
that gives away her tiniest mistakes.

She completes the set.
She bows as if the ancestors
were lined up before her.
In the instant when her eyes are looking downward,
Master Liang places himself where the ancestors would be.
He does this with no visible movement.
When Ana has straightened again,
she lifts her eyes.
They open very wide.
Now Master Liang smiles with his eyes
and every muscle in his face.
"You are stiff," he says.
You must play with whole heart."

Ana steps into his arms
open as wide as they have ever been.
Into his shoulder she weeps
exactly as if she were a little girl.

Sword Form

~ *for Sifu Ray Hayward*

The sword in its scabbard —
iron and carbon refined to purest steel —
holds a promise of deep reward:
to those who practice, insight revealed.

Hand cherishes the sword it holds
in firm, yet gentle, three-finger grip.
Sword clarifies mind and heart, molds
through eye-gaze focused solely on the tip.

Sword brings whole body to its form.
To cut or slice, the waist must turn.
A stab or thrust is *chi* through legs transformed.
Before issue, one must first the target earn.

With tassel, waist and legs propel the movement,
while wrist directs to hit, block or disarm.
In two-person, sword targets the opponent,
not mere sword-on-sword-play charm.

Thirteen energies lay the foundation
for T'ai-Chi and Wu-Tang sword.
Each posture names a specific station
along the Taoist journey forward.

Steel is crafted to sword, its temper
a blending of heat, coolness, and time.
So, Sword Form refines its practitioner,
infusing self with self's paradigm.

Morning T'ai-Chi

Cloud hands
pull like weavers
the fine threads drawing sun
from her lazy quilt of starlight
to work.

Bat

Window,

open unseen.

A bat sweeps through the room,

sounding. A benediction for

faint hearts.

Oceans to Arches

Limestone:
filigree of
fossils, millennia
holding up ceilings. Beneath them,
sleepers.

Dicotyledon

Pin oak,
sharp as holly,
confiscating all the light.
You leave your cousins to spread the
shadows.

Empty Stepping

Standing
is not enough,
my here so far from there.
Full, I cannot move. Shift. Toe out.
Forward.

61

Bibliography

Cheng Man-ch'ing. *Master of Five Excellences.* Translation & Commentary by Mark Hennessy. Berkeley, California: Frog, Ltd., 1995.

T'ai Chi Ch'uan: A Simplified Method of Calisthenics for Health & Self Defense. Trans. Beauson Tseng. Berkeley, California: North Atlantic Books, 1981.

Davis, Barbara, Translator & Commentator. *The Taijiquan Classics: An Annotated Translation.* Berkeley, California: North Atlantic Books, 2004.

Gallagher, Paul B. *Drawing Silk: Masters' Secrets for Successful Tai Chi Practice.* Fairview, North Carolina: Total Tai Chi, 2007.

Hayward, Ray, Editor & Compiler. *Real Gold does Not Fear the Fire: The Teachings of Grand Master Wai-lun Choi.* St. Paul, Minnesota: Shu-Kuang Press, 2008.

T'ai-Chi Ch'uan: Lessons with Master T.T. Liang. Rev. & Expanded Edition. St. Paul, Minnesota: Shu-Kuang Press, 2000.

Laotzu. *The Way of Life According to Laotzu: An American Version.* Translation by Witter Bynner in collaboration with Kiang Kang-hu. New York: Perigee Press, 1972.

Liang, Master T.T. *T'ai Chi Ch'uan for Health & Self-Defense: Philosophy & Practice.* Edited & with Foreword by Paul B. Gallagher. New York: Vintage Books, 1997.

Schorre, Jane. With calligraphy by Margaret Chang. *How to Grasp the Bird's Tail if You Don't Speak Chinese.* Berkeley, California: North Atlantic Books, 2000. 2nd printing.